Curriculum

P9-CLB-811

When Clay Sings

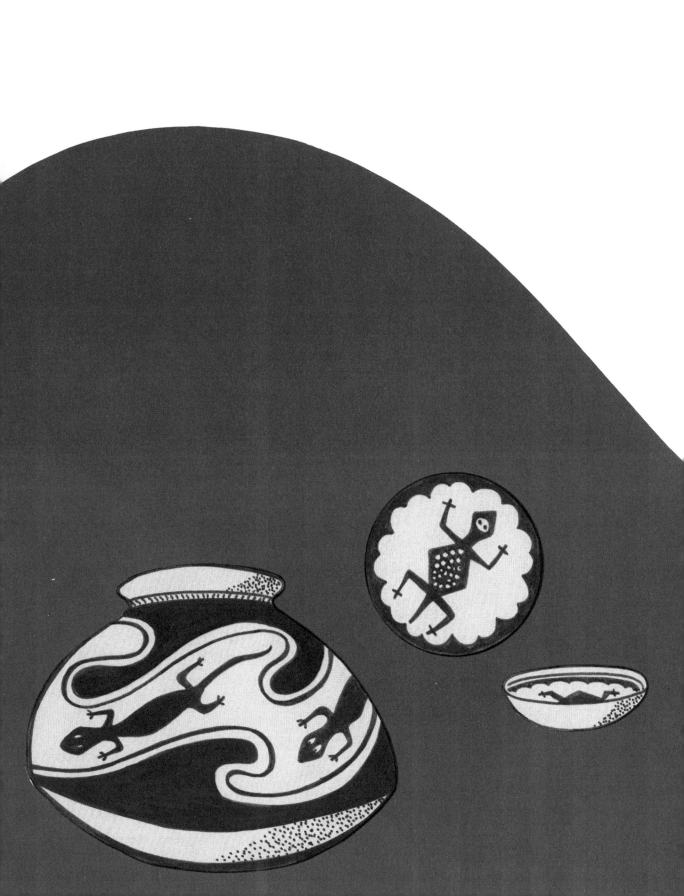

When Clay Sings

by BYRD BAYLOR

illustrated by TOM BAHTI

Published by Charles Scribner's Sons · New York

FRANKLIN PIERCE
COLLEGE LIBRARY
RINDGE, N. H. 03461

CURR.
E
78
.S7
B36
1972

Text Copyright © 1972 Byrd Baylor
Illustrations Copyright © 1972 Tom Bahti

This book published simultaneously in
the United States of America and in Canada—
Copyright under the Berne Convention

All rights reserved. No part of this book
may be reproduced in any form without
the permission of Charles Scribner's Sons.

7 9 11 13 15 17 19 RD/C 20 18 16 14 12 10 8 6

Printed in the United States of America
Library of Congress Catalog Card Number 70-180758
SBN 684-12807-1 (Trade cloth, RB)

Dedicated to the ancient artists who created these designs and to the museums which preserve them

There are
desert hillsides
where
ancient
Indian pottery
still lies
half buried
in the sand
and
lizards
blink at
other dusty lizards
that were painted
on those pots
a thousand years ago.

Now
Indian children
make a game
of searching for
bits of
clay
that were once
somebody's
bowl
or mug
or cooking pot
or dipper.

Their parents
look at what
they find
and tell them:

"Remember, treat
it with respect.
It is so old. . . ."

They say
that every piece
of clay
is a piece of
someone's
life.

They even say
it has
its own
small voice
and sings in
its own way.

So
the children
touch
the pieces
carefully
as they
kneel there
in the hot
dry sand
listening
for whatever
voice
a broken pot
might use—

A windy voice?
A sandy voice?
A voice like
a far bird's
cry?

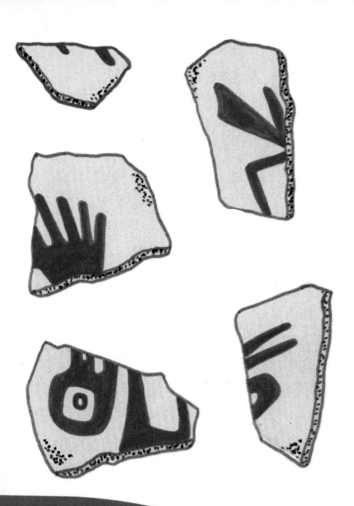

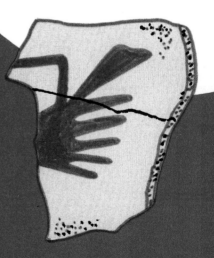

Sometimes
if they look long enough
and
if they are lucky enough
they can fit
four
or
five
pieces
together
the way you'd do
a jigsaw puzzle.

Then
suddenly
they see
a perky
wide-eyed
bird
look up
at them . . .

surprised.

Maybe
the bowl
with the bird
was dropped
by some other
Indian child
who chased
a rabbit
near these same rocks
then.

When they find
a bowl
that isn't broken
the children can
pretend
that they've just
eaten from it
and that
they're sitting
by some campfire
on a deerskin blanket
and it's
then
not
now

and
they speak
an older
language.

But
they don't need words
to know
that there were
speckled bugs
and spotted bugs
and bugs with
shiny wings
and pinchy bugs
and jumpy bugs
and bugs that had
a thousand legs
that liked to walk
through grass . . .

They know
the molding of
a lump of clay
has always been
a slow
and gentle
work.
No hurrying.
No rushing.

Hands that
shape
the earth
this way
have time
to know
the cool
touch
of the sand.

Women then
must have
spoken
to the earth
as they took
its clay.
They must have
sung special
songs
for shaping the bowl,
for polishing it,
for baking it
so it would be
strong enough
to last
long after
that tribe
was gone. . . .

Once
somebody
sitting on the ground
outside a high
cold
cliffhouse
thought:
"I'll make
this bowl
as pretty
as I can."

And she painted
what she
liked
the most . . .

stars
and moon
and sun

and whirlwinds.

Was the sun shining
as she worked?
Were her own
brown
naked children
playing near?
Was there a
skinny dog?
Was the smell
of cooking
in the air?
Did a man
come back from
hunting
and shake his head?

And on another day
did she
paint
that hunter
too?

Sometimes
children
may have
said:
(but in that
other language)

"Mama, make
a bowl
with pictures
of big animals
for me . . .
big
fierce
creatures
that I'll
hunt someday."

So
she drew
mountain lions
and wildcats
and

even a man
wrestling
a bear.

Or
is it
a bear
wrestling
a man?

The colors
are
still bright–

Reds as deep as
sandstone cliffs,
browns and tans
the shade of
desert earth,
black and white

shiny as
stones
polished
by water
in high
mountain streams.

There were a
thousand
shapes to draw—

Horned toads
and lizards.
Butterflies.
Turtles.
And beautiful
leaping fish.

And deer
and mountain goats
and antelope
that flashed
across
these canyons

always
faster than
the boys
who knew their
trails
and followed them
among the rocks.

They even drew
the
scariest
things
they could
think of.
Call them
monsters.
Call them
night spirits.
Call them
anything.

Children
make them up
today
and they
still have
the same
scarey look
in their eyes.

Many a child
must have eaten
rabbit stew
for supper
out of bowls
with rabbits
painted on them.

what rabbit
couldn't
jump
through
that hole
in the dish?

Here's a hunter
who used
a fine long net
for catching
rabbits . . .
but

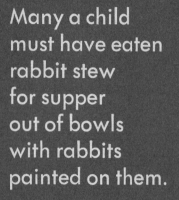

This child
was sick
and they called
a medicine man
to cure him.

What magic
is he using?

What special
chants
and dances
and whispered words
and feathered wands
may have helped
a boy
get well again?

And
did medicine
made from
dry roots
and flowers
and wild
yellow grasses
taste
like
pink medicine
tastes now?

Indians who find
this pottery today
say
that everything
has its own
spirit—
even a broken pot.

They say
the clay
remembers
the hands
that made it.

Does it
remember
the cornfields too?
And the
summer rains?
And the
ceremonies
that held
life together?

Here are
the masks
and the
costumes

and the
great
dancing
figures.

Here is the
flute player
bent low
over his
song.

Songs
had to be
powerful
enough
to make
rain fall
and winds
blow
and seeds
sprout
in the dark
earth....

Songs
had to be
powerful
enough
to keep

warriors safe
and lead the
hunter
to the deer
and make
summer always
follow
winter
and hold
the sun in its
proper path
across the sky

and keep life
moving on
from tribe
to
tribe.

They say
that even now
the wind sometimes
finds
one of those songs
still in the clay
and lifts it out
and carries it
down the canyon
and across
the hills.

It is a small sound
and always far away

but
they say
sometimes
they hear it.

Designs used in this book are all derived from prehistoric Indian pottery from the American Southwest. The original work was done by ancient potters of the Anasazi, Mogollon, Hohokam and Mimbres cultures.

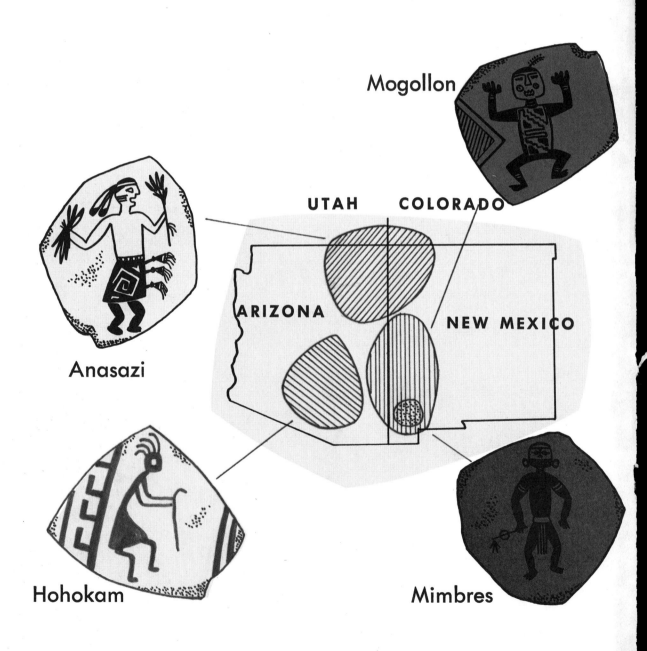

Mogollon

Anasazi

UTAH   COLORADO

ARIZONA   NEW MEXICO

Hohokam

Mimbres